This book Belongs to

_____

Dear colorist,

When I set out to draw the artwork for this book, I wanted to place my chibi characters in unusual settings, rather than just stick with the comic style perspective backgrounds that are common with this style of artwork. I thought of the nature of chibis—cute and mischievous—and wanted the finished pictures to reflect that personality. I had so much fun creating this book for you and I hope that you will have just as much fun coloring it in.

I hand draw my images the old fashioned way, with a black fine liner pen and white paper. I do not use a computer to render my images. There is just something special about a truly hand drawn picture, and I love using my art supplies. There are lines that are a bit uneven and shaky, there are circles that are not perfectly round. Everything you see in this book came from my hand, directly—so the lines are not computer perfect, and that is what makes my drawings original.

Relax and have a good time coloring. You deserve some time just for you!

Best wishes and thank you for buying this color book—Ionia

Test your colors here:

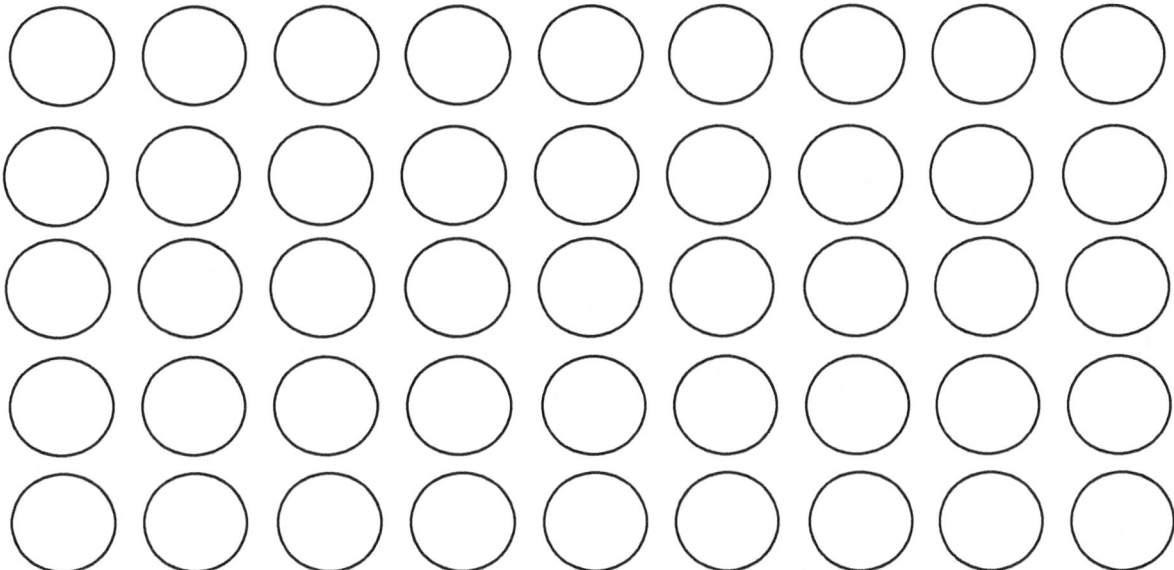

Cut out this page and insert behind the page you are currently coloring.